Black Dog Happy

poems by

Danny Berardinelli

Finishing Line Press
Georgetown, Kentucky

Black Dog Happy

Respect in the animal an active intellect:
Each flower is a soul in Nature bloomed forth…

"Golden Lines," Gerard De Nerval (tr. Robert Duncan)

Copyright © 2017 by Danny Berardinelli
ISBN 978-1-63534-203-1 First Edition
All rights reserved under International and Pan-American Copyright Conventions.
No part of this book may be reproduced in any manner whatsoever without written permission from the publisher, except in the case of brief quotations embodied in critical articles and reviews.

Publisher: Leah Maines

Editor: Christen Kincaid

Cover Art: Danny Berardinelli

Author Photo: Dennis Hayzaik

Cover Design: Elizabeth Maines McCleavy

Printed in the USA on acid-free paper.
Order online: www.finishinglinepress.com
also available on amazon.com

Author inquiries and mail orders:
Finishing Line Press
P. O. Box 1626
Georgetown, Kentucky 40324
U. S. A.

Table of Contents

White Wolf Dream 1
Black Dog Happy 2
Poem at 3 in the Morning 3
Raccoon Rite 4
Pigs Must Die 5
Survival of the Fittest 6
The Naming of Things 7
The Nature of Things 8
Animal Anxious 9
PETA Paraphrase 10
Animal Rescue 11
Olfactory Disruptions 12
Busy Busy People 13
Museum of the Cherokee 14
Business as Usual 15
A Day at the Cleveland Zoo 16
White Bawana Wears Elevator Shoes 17
Animal Anxious 2 18
Quartet 19
Brown Bag Lunch 21
The Day Romero Died 22
Ticket to Heaven 23
Funny Farm 24
Happy Trails to You 25
State of Emergency 26
Making Do 27
The Uffizi Dancers 28
The Greatest Generation 29
Canto Hondo 30
Woman Without Tears 31
In the Watchfires 32
Curly Howard Plays Hamlet 33
Bureau of Employment Services 34
Puncture Points 35
Sad-Sack Moon 36
Life in Captivity: Dolphins 37
Life in Captivity: Husband and Wife 38

White Wolf Dream
    (for Patty)

All-night Arctic Express
streaks across the Great Lakes,
snow drifts up our sliding door,
crystals creep down the glass.
In the morning she says:
    I try to remember
    a dream I have—
    it slips beneath
    my sleep
    and the comforter
    we keep
    for coldest nights
    and all I've got
    to go on
    is a white wolf
    leaving hunks of meat
    on the patio...
then she puts her head with mine
on the pillow...*catch-if-catch-can,*
    my white wolf dream.

Black Dog Happy
    (for Pedro)

Black dog happy is.
Likes to wear silly
jingle-jingle cap—
we laugh, we laugh.
Pedro, he is, who is
Maker of fun and games.
Yes he is who is.
See, Danny, see black dog
drop fuzzy bright balls
in Mommy's clean clothes,
bury like bones
in deep, puffy snow
(doggy looks down,
doggy looks up, down.
up, and then, at last,
Danny gets the point).
Fuzzy ball comes
 off the wall,
on the fly...Pedro, catch!
goes plop on the pool,
swim, swim...Danny, fetch!

Poem at 3 in the Morning

On the first day, Lao Tzu fed the monkeys
4 nuts in the morning, 3 nuts late
that afternoon.
It made the monkeys hoot and holler.
On the second day, Lao reversed himself:
3 nuts in the morning and 4 to follow up.
The monkeys all were grateful.
This is called 3 in the morning
In the *Book of the Way*—
in monkey terms:
"working within the system."

Raccoon Rite (a true story)
> *The animal looks at us and we are naked before it.* —Jacques Derrida

Wide-eyed as Jake, I'm
   braking for a turn
off S.R. 48, dumbstruck by raccoons
roadside—one strokes another's carcass—

hairs bristle, neck and arms, when,
tragic in its dark mask, it gazes back
at me and

stretches out her twiggy foreleg
in that familiar gesture we call:
supplication.

Thirty years and still her gaze
sticks in me

like the face on St. Veronica's veil.

Pigs Must Die
    (another true story)

Funding has been cut and pigs are all infected.
Not to worry. There's bound to be a gizmo and a
fix. Consult the protocols…there it is:
lethabarb injections all around. Stoke the furnace.
Load the carts. Soon we're almost home-free
when this little piggy turns trickster, plays possum,
wiggles down into the heap.
                                            Mere contiguity
(Professors all agree); not to be confused
with intentions, affections, or fancies that impede
                           the March of Progress.

Survival of the Fittest

Long, long ago,
some little lizards took to leaping
and foreleg tissue, up to then
an obstacle to creeping, shot
them up and far away from
great big lizards and their
great big heads
that were mostly jaws and teeth.

The Naming of Things

        Fear of falling's one thing.
Here's another. A precipice
In Utah where everything is bent
on playing tricks. Canyon
ocean-deep, horizon-wide. My gaze
goes crazy-god-like. A twisty
juniper leans out beside me
as if it would uproot itself and fly away.
      I watch my step, stiff-backed
knees knocking
and fill myself with Zion.
      Later, down below,
in a dried-up Virgin River bed,
tiny lizards scramble over ripple marks,
flash like minnows in our cool Ohio creeks.
      Natives called it "Waken"
Press and Pulp, "The Badlands,"
Mormons gave it Bible names—
              all of which sound
              equally improper
              when spoken by a Juniper
              hovering on the abyss.

The Nature of Things

Whatever you call it, the Nature of Things
is mostly floating on magma,
slip-sliding on fault-lines.

At old *Euclid Beach*, Dad and I rode
The Flying Turns and *Racing Coasters*,
Over-the-Falls and *Thriller*,
all except the *Rotor*.
Like Lucretius on the rocks
we oversaw it all from the catwalk.
On the metal catwalk we could watch
(just below our Summer shoes),
the rotating sons and daughters of
the Proletariat.
> *Hurry…hurry! Step this way and see!*
> *the round room twirl, accelerate. In the*
> *blink of an eye, the round floor drops.*
> *And then, behold, some folk stick,*
> *some slip…*

it's just the Nature of things; but, here's the trick—

those who stick stand
stiff-backed, chin high, still as
still can be; those who fall…
they twitch, shift a leg, an arm,
twist their necks—refuse surrendering
to centrifugal force.

Animal Anxious

        Because they don't have souls
(according to the Know-It-Alls)
I'm supposed to Man-Up.
Nonetheless, to me, it's a matter
of concern. Each April,
a pair of Canada geese appear.
They nest atop a mound of dirt and
dead grass in the wet-land run-off
East of KSU.

But just today, a solitary goose
stands roadside, staring at the mound
in its seasonal disrepair. Now, bless me
Father, I confess, it's on my mind
and will be on my mind until
the day that I drive by and spot
one goose nesting, one on guard.

PETA Paraphrase

Her name was Double Trouble,
this tabby cat of orange,
victim of a research grant
at Wisconsin U.
Stainless-steel screwed
into her skull, toxins dripped
into her ears and, of course,
electrodes in her brain (what
good can come if not for those
electrodes in her brain?).
All proceeded as it should
until she woke from surgery,
paralyzed (imagine that).
"Afterwards, she seemed depressed"
(go figure). Nothing to be done:
"too sick to be useful." So, they
cut off her head, sliced up her brain,
and then pronounced it all a failure.
Funny thing:
results were never published.

Animal Rescue

Breaking News! On satellite from India!
Hindus throw dead pig
into Moslem prayer group….
Riots leave 13 dead…
Hundreds injured!…

Who, oh who, will rescue them?
 from Myths and fables and
dietary principles, protocols of cleanliness,
Godliness, Cartesian double-talk—and save us
from ourselves, all our fantasies of werewolf, vampire,
cloven-hoof Mephisto (no, no…Mephisto is a
Gentleman!)?

Tonight, dew-drenched lilacs
through an open window
clear my head; images appear
of animals I've known:
one-legged robin hopping after worms,
three-legged coon raiding garbage cans,
Shelley cat, surviving cancer on three legs,
squirreling into apple trees…

one eyed, sway-back, tortoise-shell,
Skeeter the Speeder, tossed roadside
but now living big, leaping up to slap
our potted ivy on her pedestal…
golden, long-haired Trixie cat
whose green sparkle eyes
conceal her wasting retinas
and still she roams through mental maps
of furnished rooms with frequent
touch and sometime bumps upon
her little noggin…

Jerry Terrier, failing as a show-dog
after a botched debarking,
short of breath but long on grunts
and always up for running, swimming,
howling in squeak-toy *falsetto*…
and polydactyl Mr. Claws, Zeno cat
on weekly fluid drips, stub-tail
Katy cat, on the lam from bully boys.
abandoned and neglected, dismembered and
disfigured—see how they thrive!

Never, never more
will I resort to metaphors
from bestiaries, bibles, and learned books
and all such primitive works of man.

Olfactory Disruptions

Raked up with the Autumn leaves
in the bed of annuals today, darker
odors of anise, like a sudden whiff
of perfume, when nobody is there…
and I'm up in the all night,
sorting through junk drawers,
burning letters, bagging mementos
for the morning trash.

Busy Busy People

...on a busy, busy holiday...full of travel
from the East side to the Park...
(it's all for the kids of course)
at the Zoo

where kids are flipping peanuts to Grizzlies...
at the Zoo,

tots are playing knock-knock
on White Boa's window...
in the middle of things
at the Zoo,

Cleveland's Great Ape
catches fragrance of hot dogs,
cotton candy and sweat
in Summer breeze, above
and all around this
busy busy holiday...

Museum of the Cherokee

1. Up from wrecks
of American chestnuts
apple tree grows wildwood tall.
On rim trail, gravel strips
are all that's left of the railroad.
These scattered chips
were garden walks:
heart-a-burst stirring in a cold spot.

2. In and out of morning mist,
forest flies, ridges
break, deer and bear appear,
disappear—shifting shape.
Half-way to Double-Springs,
high on a hemlock ridge,
a solitary tombstone, hard
to spot: Sally Sutton, 18,
always looking West.
One name, one date, overlooking
valleys and coves and
a couple-thousand unmarked graves.

3. Oconaluftee sings
in many tongues
as if the day had never been
(will never be)
when Jackson thumbs his nose
at the Black-Robes
and Major Ridge
signs the straight line
on a crooked treaty.
Removal begins.
Lotteries and auctions.
Pots and pans and
purple beads, gone
with the wind.
All because they came…
those so-called settlers
with allotments
and a slender, cottony fungus.

4. At the gas station,
Black Bear paces
round and round
a chain-link pen, or,
to everyone's amusement,
takes a dip in a claw-leg
bathtub, under a BP sign.

Business as Usual

At Greasy Grass
the women shoved their needles
into Custer's ear:
"Can you hear us now,
Son of the Morning Star?"
But we just kept on plowing
grasslands, carving Teddy
(spectacles and all)
into blocks of Black Hill.

A Day at the Cleveland Zoo

It was a rite of Spring
for Mom and me.
The bus dropped us off at
Broadview Bridge
for the long, precipitous
walk into Cuyahoga valley.
We pass the old brickyard—
gaping furnace red with rust,
rotting pallets, stacks of crumbling
bricks wrapped in grape vines,
sprouting iron weed—"Grandpa
worked in brickyards," Mamma
always says.

We passed the scary Metro Pool
where Mom, when just a kid herself,
swam fearlessly. I was more for blue,
suburban rectangles
not this Black Lagoon. What awful
shovels must have dug the earth so wide,
so round and deep?

At hippo's house, we wait and wait,
(not like people at the zoo but patiently
as hunters do) until the water bubbles
and she breaks—
Leviathan from the deep.

Then onward to the cathouse where Tigers pace
and sunbeams strike between the trees;
Tiger leaps on iron bars, fearful paws
that give the lie to White Bawana
wrestling big cats on the silver screen.
A breeze blows shadow leaves
swirling on the concrete floor and
Tiger spins, pounces, spins again
as kitties do with feather toys.

By dinner time, I'm napping on the bus,
home to bungalows and tree-lawns
and dreams of jungle nights where
fiery eyes are burning, night birds calling…
dreams so deep they seem more like
a memory.

White Bawana Wears Elevator Shoes

Today I learned a thing or two
about the Zoo.
Menagerie days are done—
the "naked cage" no more.
The Zoo reforms itself:
the "Living Museum"
where honey locust mimics acacia,
synthetic Serengeti.

Gone are the snows of Kilimanjaro!
Gone is the coral in the deep blue sea!—
but White Bawana lives in an old movie.
In a black lagoon, Quiet Man wrestles
man-eating octopus, big as all outdoors
but still no match for hyper-action ego.

Don't you almost envy it?—that
Greatest Generation, with land, lots of
land. Never was heard a discouraging
word; but they sang and they sang
all over the dam: "Don't fence me in!"

Animal Anxious Number 2

"A wounded deer leaps highest"
as the front end of my Chevy proves.
A deer rockets moonward
then crashes in a roadside ditch
with a dreadful, hollow thud, followed
by a rustle of dry grass. Then silence,
cold as Autumn moonbeams.

Days after, when I pass, the stench shames
me and I curse my car and I curse
the thousands it took to repair.

Then, early in May, near a gulley where
Lover's Lane crosses Infirmary,
a fawn appears, curled on a bed of grass
still as a *Bradford* collectible.

I'm glad, of course, but nonetheless I wonder,
where's Mama?

QUARTET: THE SWEETEST MUSIC THIS SIDE OF HEAVEN

Working bare-knuckled, without a net—like boys and chimpanzees
electro-bio-chemically fused, soon-to-be released by *Universal
Pictures,*
          Dave and Ricky, Jack [and me] climbing
hand-over-hand girders up backsides of billboards, higher than
telephone lines and trees so we can see across Brookpark where
train tracks run and ragged hoboes chase disobedient little boys.
Perched above it all, our gaze extends to Terminal Tower and
out over sparkling Lake Erie where make-believe Godzilla rises.

          Once, some neighbors driving by
spotted boys on high and all of us caught hell. Dad could let slide:
You want him to be a sissy? But Mom would have us play it safe
not at all like jazz on rainy nights; more like top-ten pop
beating four to every bar.

          But what's a mom to do about
bullies on Brookpark? Their mothers pack the PTA, fathers stack
City Council, serve in "Altar and Rosary." It's really up to me
to stand my ground, draw mental maps of side-streets, back-yards,
every kind of fence (chain-link, picket, wood or wire)—
befriend all neighborhood dogs.

And what's a mom to do, when her one and only needs a
nightlight, though she'd have him sleeping like a man,
alone in the dark? Cancel that subscription to *Creepy
Magazine*? Forbid the Sunday matinee? Still each night
he's on alert for Wolfman crossing Little Creek or
Rue Morgue chimp come crashing through the window.

And still there'd be the nightly news:
Beverly Jarosz, murdered in her father's house,
fifteen minutes down the road… still there'd be
little Chubby in the schoolyard, red-face and hair
like cactus needles, mouth stretched in a wet
grin, as he grabbed my balls at recess…still there'd be
the organist at Church who squeezed my thigh, and then
that little incident in Dealey Plaza.

And what's a latch-key kid to do on a Summer day when
the phone rings, a gravel-voice growls: "Are you
home? Good.... Santa's coming early this year."
When dark shadows stain the curtain, the knock seems
to buckle the door, and my guardian collie, Major,
is just too old and weak to bark. No, no, not all the crew-cut
lawns and sidewalks of suburbia will keep the monsters out.

By May 4, 1970, my nightlight was history and
all I had to fear was Ohio's National Guard.
Darkness…eh…I embraced it
like any other fact of life, foregone conclusion…
like boys will be boys, like chimps are chimps and
bullies must bully and the twain shall never meet.
                                        Still, it doesn't mean that
every now and then, a dot dropped in common time
can't make dull boys shine—even if they never know
how they figure in serial adventures, how legend longing burns,
especially on rainy nights, gutters gushing down the spouts,
rushing into river songs that only I can hear
                                        on the sunny side of sleep.

Brownbag Lunch

always makes me blue
homesick and dyspeptic
eating on the clock
like piece-work
cold cuts, cola, pickle
all kinds of piece-meals
and a plastic pudding-cup
and no matter how thinly shaved
the ham (is there really a Bavaria
or just a "conspiracy of cartographers")
and no matter how many *Hershey* kisses,
 (is there nothing more shocking than
a bit of foil crushed against a silver filling?)
and no matter how sunny and warm
on the park bench....
brownbag lunch
always makes me feel
I'm a sad little man
in a great big brownbag country.

The Day Romero Died (another brownbag day)
> *You are suffering like Christ on the cross.*
> *So Jesus must be kissing you.*   —Mother Teresa

At Fordham and Georgetown and even
Fort Bennington, Roman Catholics like to sing:
> *The Lord hears the cry of the poor,*
> *Blessed be the Lord...*

Down El Salvador way,
another careless priest spills the cup
in his own blood...
meanwhile,
back at the ranch, double-barreled
Buckley cracks vernacular:
> *That's what they get*
> *when they pussyfoot*
> *with Communists.*

Kirkpatrick at the UN
blames nuns for running guns
to (who else?) communists.
Meanwhile, back at the ranch,
the Polish Pope is silent—
"Solidarity" stops at the border.

From Carmel to Calcutta,
Mother flies
> *faster   than a speeding bullet...*

but not so fast as bullets in the belfry
where Father Carranza dies,
bleeding-out like gangsters on St. Valentine's...
and the children of Aguilares sing:
> *No one hears the cry of the poor*
> *or the sound of a wooden bell.*

Ticket to Heaven

    Remember the day
when Jesse's brother
made us roll our eyes, right
here on the front porch.
He was sprawling
and fidgeting on the threadbare sofa,
staring off into fresh-plowed fields
when he mumbled,
  "Damn…another summer wasted
      in this hole."
Then he went to war
and got blasted into somewhere
that his mother calls
      "A Better Place…."

Funny Farm

Abandoned barns mostly fade to gray, buckle then
collapse. This one ripples, shivers in its timbers,
like a ship on stormy seas. Alone, in a field
long neglected, boards all sun-bleached to an
odd coral brightness, it turns my head each time
I pass Mennonite on Infirmary. It plays loose
with Mormon whitewash, Amish angles.
To Granny's home-grown pie, pappy's home-baked
steers, worksheets and bedshirts flapping on a line,
to all the other brummagem of local color, I say,
so What? But one old barn takes a hell of turn in a
home-town field and…well…I just keep looking into it
like a poet with his empty purse.

Happy Trails to You

Cold night hiking
on the Appalachian trail…
on a night like this
long ago and far away
Franz Liszt came knocking,
knuckle to monastic door….
fingers formed to flash
melodies and harmonies
clenched against the wood,
no strings attached.
It's a strange case, indeed, when music
fails to please and all across the scowling page,
figures putrefy like the body of Mr. Valdemar—
until there's nothing left
but dark of night, trees groaning…
"What is it you seek, seignior?"
"Serenity."

State of Emergency
> *...only a fool's help is real help.* —Walter Benjamin

4 and 20 white boys
baked in Mommy's pie
take a break from stomping gays
to kick an ash-gray kitten in the park;
little boys and girls scream,
parents spirit them to Mommy Vans
but then, like an angel dropped into
suburbia, a one-armed man, on his
way to mail a worker's claim,
steps between, bends low, calls her
"Smokey" slowly, gently scoops her up
with one hand.

Making Do

Sorry, old piano. Banished to the cellar
fifteen years without a tuning,
worn pads, broken strings, and G below
middle C that sticks for measures at a time.
Poor Elise! stumbling over sixteenths
as she climbs the old *Knabe*,
decades out of production.
Beer stains on the upper octave,
scorched pot seeds underneath.
Pandora's Box of bad dreams, of
keyboards without cracks that
make nothing come but flop-sweat.

Yet every now and then, the spirit blows up
white-water arpeggios, effortless turns and trills;
and presto, I appear—god from the machine,
until…of course…G below middle C.

The Uffizi Dancers (a true story)

> *Hanging from a gallows by one foot was a medieval custom known as baffling.* —Barbara G. Walker, Secrets of the Tarot

The story goes (or went) like this: Andrea del Sarto
meant to execute some dancers—in rustic pose—
life-sized and motley—working from these sketches
            that prove to be, instead,
of hanged men:
                  debtors, murderers, and thieves.
Shock of hair, lock of knee, told of their disaster
       when, at last, some curious curator found
up was really down.
Take it as a lesson on the hazards of intention:
           Play gypsy play!
tumbles into *just another Dance of Death.*

The Greatest Generation

"We're the ones who saved the world,
followed orders, believed what we were told:
yellow men and monkeys
live in tress, can't fly planes—
believed it all, up until that morning
at Pearl Harbor."

Then my father brought his photo album down
from the high shelf I couldn't reach
and pointed to a picture that he took on
Bougainville. Muddle of disconnected arms,
torsos, heads—strange, other things—bulldozed
into earth. Ancient, silent forest all around.

"This is Hill 700. This is war," he said,
"not some John Wayne movie. And here's
that goddamn McArthur in his goddamn jeep
script in hand. Back and forth from surf to shore—
take one…two…three—each time claiming victory:
'I will return!' Sure, when it's over, he'll return.
Hell, he saw more action at Tent City.

"Now this…this one here, is New Zealand
where we built a bridge of mahogany—
the trees there were all mahogany.
Dan, you never saw anything more beautiful."

The Oracle of Delphi long ago revealed that
Telemachus wrote *The Odyssey*. And why not?
A father's voice gets in your head, never lets you
rest assured that heritage or history
will dare to tell
how the warriors let the wind out of the bag.

Canto Hondo

                First person singular rises like a triumph cry, like
                columns of regular design, finished as a final sum
                        but everything
                        on earth resorts
                        to deep songs;
                        quiet streets of
                        Andalusia where
                        old wooden bells
                        three times clap,
                        one dark-skinned
                        contadora offers
          up her song, sun-struck on a balcony, one articulate
hand on the iron rail arrested, like patience on a monument, not
at all a player in a play; and people in the streets below, bow their heads—
remember…odors of Moorish gardens on moonlit nights…or else, perhaps,
they're wishing for the wretched earth to quake, crack, and wake the faithful
                                dead.

Woman without Tears
> *Non piangere.* —Anna Banti

I'll tell you what Rome was like in those days…
and how she came to pull the master's beard.

In those days, she couldn't open windows
without some jerk giving her the finger
so she hid herself behind the easel,
her initials in the shadow of Susanna's leg.

She won the praise of all but Volteranno
who had his way with her naked figure
of "Desire." With his own brush, he
dressed it up in robes like a Madonna.
*After all, the sons of Buonarroti must not
scandalized.*

And even though her maid did the baking—
You must not ruin your hands, Mistress!—
it was the maid who left a door unlocked
for Agostino:

As Agostino bursts into her room
she's painting for her own delight;
>*No more painting! Girl!*
>*No more painting!*

When he leaves, she throws her pallet knife
but only draws a spot of blood.

No one frets about her hands
when the jailors use their thumbscrews
and force her to recant.

After that, she paints with wild resolve:
Judith come to spill the tyrant's blood
with the tyrant's own sword, her trustworthy
maid beside her, a knee on Holofernes' chest
to hold him down.

Deflowered now, this girl
who painted delicate bouquets, mixes colors
with wormwood to make herself an object of
her own desire.

"In the watch fires..."

> *the zeal often rises in proportion to the error...*   —David Hume

When that chubby rat appeared
overhead in red-tail hawk talons
as I crossed the parking lot,
I thought of you old Aristander,
Alexander's oracle, trying all your
wits to make the murder seem legit,
how Alexander makes you tremble
on the west bank of the Ganges
when a soldier dares to sneeze...
"the court swarmed with sacrifices—
purifiers, prognosticators...."
the field erupts with
Greek Fire and White Phosphorus...
the holy man blesses the boys
Theoclymenus and Billy Graham...
By this Sign You Conquer...Venus victrix!

And Plutarch records that
even Augustus was "extremely uneasy"
on the morning of a bloodbath, "when he
happened to put the right shoe on his left foot."

Curly Howard Plays Hamlet in the NUT
(the New Utopian Theater…yuk, yuk yuk)

"What a piece of work is man…."
And what a piece of slapstick
this prince absorbed (in secret parts)
by something in a book, while Providence
or Fate or Daddy's Girl sets him up
for pratfall, center-stage.
That's the whole thing in a nutshell:
to come and go oblivious, altogether
in ourselves like plants and other
animals, without anticipation.
That's the trick *in the woild,*
soi'nly—ta play the Stooge—
Emperor Octopus Grabus.
And not to saw the air too much,
whirling round a passion
like that fire-breathing Baptist
and poisonous polemicist
all frothy on the *Fox News—*
each Himself, the Paragon of Animals,
King, by Cock, of Infinite Space!

Employment Services

> *...to write is to renounce being in command of oneself.*
> —Maurice Blanchot, *The Writing of the Disaster*

We are the people of the Bureau.
Not the Bureau people. That's different.
It's only here that we combine, stinking of
cigarettes and fear; and though we lean together,
our heads are not hollow.
Some of us read books. My copy of *Inferno* wears
a greasy finger-print at line 112, Canto 19.
We come to file claims, appeal claims denied.
This guy with a resume is standing at the wrong desk.
The clerk redirects him to another desk...end of the line.
I want to be nice, speak an encouraging word,
something nice about his resume which no one
here will care about.   But I'm busy
looking at a pretty girl. She's explaining
how her right arm was crushed in a punch-press.
And I'm busy hoping that all our moving parts survive
another round of working...and not working.

PUNCTURE POINTS

1. A man's reach, a man's grasp,
and what's a heaven for—don't
they love it: spitting in the wind,
those Great Men in their Great
Books. If lightning bolts and
thunder rolls, they spout metaphors
Me, I run for cover and an old
memory revives, my wife's
not my own.
Exploring with her friend,
on a morning after violent storms,
they came upon an old white workhorse
scorched on his beautiful hide, dead
among some fallen maples where
he thought to hide.

2. Hauling out recycling,
in darkness before dawn,
head hung low, full of things
to do, plan to do, even want to do
caught up in all my crazy counting
 (one chore, two chores, wind the
clock and more), when,
what dumb luck…I'm dumbstruck!
to just that moment raise my eyes, that very
second it was passing: a meteor
coming down,
burning brightly, brightly,
as…well…a meteor.

Sad-Sack Moon

> *They sentenced me to twenty years of boredom*
> *trying to change the system from within....* —Leonard Cohen

Tonight, I've been thinking about another night
when a friend said about a poem of mine: "It takes a lot of
balls to poke fun at God like that."
So I changed the title and two offensive lines, but finally
just deleted the whole damn thing; but not for the reason
that my friend believed (though I thanked him for his sound
advice). Reason was, it's not about my "balls," not that
Terrible Love of Combat.

Convinced he never could surpass Vivaldi, Giuseppe Torelli
threw himself from the window of his loft. He took a lucky bounce
and lived to write and play again and more than that, as *Schirmer's
Pocket Manual* tells, to shine again. *Giuseppe Torelli: originator of
the solo violin concerto.*

And now tonight, in my half-moon window, a full yellow moon
is hanging low, like me, and I just go on thinking of all my
deletions. Oh, I was riding high, until I read in Brontë,
my own fake longings in a voice that rang true: "I wish I could see
how the ocean is lashing." *Anne Brontë: minor poet.*

Tonight, moon and me fess up—I free those Canada geese
I've been stuffing into odes (Horatian), quit counting syllables
on four or five fingers. Why bother? Those silly geese always beat
me to the punch, signing heaven with a "V," as Audubon explains,
to maximize every goose's range of sight.
Tonight I let it go. Embrace my incredible shrinking self,
and resign from the Visionary Company that never really wanted
me around. It's just too hard to keep it up these days, knowing
for a fact that someone years ago jammed a flag into the moon,
that moon of our fathers, and all the night-songs ever since must
screw their mouths up to a golf ball and memorial plaque.

Life in Captivity: Dolphins

> *In captivity, they are prone to neurotic behaviors—*
> *such as swimming in endless circles....*   —Naomi Rose, PhD

Swim...turn...
swim again and
click the wall
and always clicks
come back
like bolts out of the blue.
Flipper, Flipper,
faster than lightning...
in-a-bottle-lightning
click, clack...tick-tock...
ready to receive
signals from the lost pod.
May as well be scanning
for transmissions
from a distant galaxy.

Life in Captivity: Husband and Wife

Rise and shine,
toe the line,
nose to the grind…
look sharp.
One thing after another…
before you know it,
day is done.
Still, don't you wonder
how often Hymen groans in us,
Orpheus aches like a phantom limb?

www.ingramcontent.com/pod-product-compliance
Lightning Source LLC
LaVergne TN
LVHW041551070426
835507LV00011B/1033